Shine your little light

have a nice
day   love candace

MY NAME IS NOT MONKEY GIRL
Author Miriam L. Jacobs
Illustrated by Cheryl R. Derocher

Shine your little light

This Book Belongs to:

_____

I am Beautiful in Every Single Way

DEDICATION:

FOR CANDACE, OUR PRIDE AND JOY, WHO CONTINUES TO TEACH TOLERANCE AND LOVE TO EVERYONE TO WHOM SHE MEETS. MAY YOU CONTINUE TO SHINE YOUR LITTLE LIGHT.

HI. MY NAME IS CANDACE
WELCOME TO MY WORLD!
MY NAME IS NOT SUE OR JANE
AND, IT SURE ISN'T MONKEY GIRL!

WHEN I WAS A LITTLE BABY
I WAS BORN WITH A MOUTH AND A NOSE
I HAVE TWO EYES AND TWO EARS
I HAVE TEN FINGERS AND TEN TOES.

I AM JUST LIKE YOU ARE
I LOVE TO PLAY AND HAVE FUN
BUT SOMETIMES CHILDREN ARE AFRAID
OF ME AND THEN THEY START TO RUN.

I JUST WANT TO BE YOUR FRIEND
BUT WHEN YOU RUN I FEEL SO SAD
I LOVE TO JUMP AND SING AND PLAY
NOT MAKE YOU FEEL SCARED OR MAD.

THERE IS SOMETHING I WANT TO SHARE
THAT WILL MAKE YOU MY SPECIAL FRIEND.
I HAVE A MARK CALLED A NEVUS
(KNEE-VIS)
THAT IS DARK AND HAS SOME HAIR.

IT DOES NOT HURT ME AT ALL.
IT WON'T RUB OFF ON TO YOU.
WE CAN LAUGH AND PLAY WITH A BALL.
WE CAN SKIP AND JUMP ROPE, TOO!

MY NAME IS CANDACE
WELCOME TO MY WORLD!
I WANT TO BE YOUR FRIEND
AND LAUGH, AND PLAY AND TWIRL!

ALL OF US ARE SPECIAL IN
OUR OWN SPECIAL WAYS.
SOME OF US CAN JUMP HIGHER
WHILE OTHERS CAN DANCE FOR DAYS.

ONE BOY MIGHT WEAR EYE GLASSES
MY FRIEND HAS FRECKLES ON HER FACE.
THAT GIRL MIGHT HAVE LONG HAIR…
BUT, WE'RE ALL FRIENDS IN THE HUMAN RACE!

PLEASE DON'T RUN AWAY BECAUSE SOMEONE
LOOKS DIFFERENT FROM YOU.
WHAT MAKES US ALL SPECIAL
ARE THE WONDERFUL THINGS WE CAN DO!

WE CAN HELP ONE ANOTHER
TO LEARN TO DO NEW THINGS,
WE CAN TEACH EACH OTHER HOW TO SLIDE
OR TAKE TURNS PUSHING THE SWINGS!

PLEASE DON'T CALL ME MONKEY GIRL
NAME CALLING IS NOT FUN.
IF YOU WANT TO ASK ME SOMETHING
PLEASE COME ASK ME... I WON'T RUN.

CANDACE WAS BORN WITH A RARE FACIAL NEVUS
1 IN MORE THAN 200,000 BABIES ARE BORN WITH THIS CONDITION.

GIANT CONGENITAL (HAIRY) NEVUS
IS A RARE SKIN DISORDER OF UNKNOWN CAUSE AND
HAS NO KNOWN CURE.

IT IS CHARACTERIZED BY ITS SIZE (GIANT)
HAPPENS AT THE TIME OF BIRTH (CONGENITAL)
CONTAINS COURSE DARK HAIR (HAIRY)
WITHIN THE MOLE OF THE SKIN (NEVUS- LATIN FOR MOLE)
NEVUS HAS POTENTIAL TO BECOME CANCER.

FOR MORE INFORMATION AND TO MAKE CONTRIBUTIONS:
NEVUS OUTREACH, INC
http://www.nevus.org

600 SE DELAWARE AVENUE, STE. 200
BARTLESVILLE, OK 74003
1 (877) 4-A-NEVUS
MARK BECKWITH, EXECUTIVE DIRECTOR

Family Album

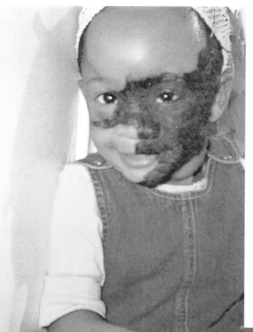

Family Album

ALL PROCEEDS FROM THE SALE OF THIS BOOK ARE FOR
CONTINUING FACIAL RECONSTRUCTION SURGERIES.

CANDACE BATTISTE SURGERY FUND

Abundant gratitude to

Dr. Bruce Bauer
Head of Plastic Surgery Children's Memorial Hospital
Chicago, Illinois

and

Dr. Amarjit Gill
Doctor of Pediatrics Monticello, New York

for your unwavering dedication to helping
Candace and all children

Author Miriam L. Jacobs

Sad Eyes

I see the sadness in her eyes.
My heart breaks when her eyes cry.
Wanting for nothing more than love
Yet, chilling when others run from her.
A child with a heart
As bright as gold;
One who loves to share her soul.
But, children fear what they don't know..
Her eyes share sadness, stories untold.
Even in school, momentary stares
Behind her back whispers and glares..
Mood swings abound, as she strives
To remain empowered.
Do adults lie?
We tell her that she's beautiful,
Smart, amazing

Yet, children say she wears ugliness
Like a dress.
I say beauty comes from within..
Radiate that beauty to those around
Let them rise to her level, inquiring
About her sad eyes and her frown.
Perhaps, then, others can learn
A thing or two about tolerance
From a child who has seen
Far too much ugliness
From children whose parents
Failed to teach that you and she
Are just like thee.
Hearts and lungs, fingers and toes
Eyes and ears, mouths and nose..
We are all the same deep inside
Please, my child, never run and hide
Because children fear what
They don't understand.
Spread your light throughout the land!
God made her in His image.
Who are we to judge and tease her?
Let those eyes smile, dry up sad tears
That their fears are unjustified
They'll know that nothing is as it
appears!
If you could walk a day in her shoes
You could not handle the constant
abuse!
Make a truce, and reintroduce
Patience and tolerance to those little feet
Who seem so happy and so carefree.
Let them know it could have been thee

Born with a difference just like she.
We as adults are the appointees
To raise compassionate, loving babies.
Teach our children what truly matters
And that staring and comparing
Is how hearts and souls shatter.

~ Miriam L Jacobs

Miriam L. Jacobs is a fallible child of God, wife, mother, grandmother, author, publisher and CEO of Candalyse Publishing.

"When Candace was born, I knew that she would change many lives. I knew that someday, I would write a book called My Name is Not Monkey Girl when a little child exclaimed,"Mommy! Look at that monkey girl!" Observing that this child's parent did nothing to teach her child that we must be compassionate and tolerant of all people, this book is intended to promote this message."

With abundant gratitude,
Miriam
www.Candalysepublishing.com
www.embracingcandace.faithweb.com

Illustrator Cheryl R. Derocher

I have plenty to say that can't wait

If you listen you may wish to join

Noise collects, sea of rhythm...

Unite

I am a poet and painter. I paint stories any way I can. Being heard is what it is all about. Letting your passion sing is the ultimate compliment so I'm looking to the future and reaching out.

"Every object to some degree is a mirror of the surrounding world. This speaks to the relationship of light acting on each living cell and natural object in a unique way. An artist must see beyond the borders of the canvas..." Cheryl Derocher

"My art is a reflection of what I think and feel. I express and explore relationships and mood through color, light atmosphere and space. I love the infinite possibilities in capturing reflections. My compositions derive order from there diagonal make up combined with the color of the foundation chosen at the outset of the project.

Choosing materials begins the process of capturing the mood or sentiment and is the key to make my work a harmonious statement of what I think or feel from the moment of its conception.

I pride myself on meeting deadlines while producing quality work. Please keep me in mind for all of your business needs. I work in many medium. Watercolor and soft sculpture are my favorites. I create in acrylics, oils and oil based ink in the block printing above.

I would love to here what you and your family love most about this book.

Contact Artist:
dererart@yahoo.com
http://derocherart.any.to

THANK YOU MIRIAM & CANDACE FOR GIFTING ME THE VOICE TO ALLOW MY ART TO SING

Draw a picture of you and Candace playing.

Draw a picture of you and Candace playing.

My Journal

_____

_____

_____

_____

_____

_____

_____

_____

My Journal

_____

_____

_____

_____

_____

_____

_____

_____

My Journal

_____

_____

_____

_____

_____

_____

_____

_____

_____

My Journal

May You Continue To

Shine your little light

Always

Candalyse Publishing Mission Statement

At Candalyse Publishing, our mission is to provide a multitude
of quality services at affordable prices to meet all of your literary needs.

We believe in the highest quality products and services
for all of our clients. We believe that our clients are our greatest
asset, and we are dedicated to serving your needs.

PleaseVisit Us On The Web
http://candalysepublishing.com

Printed in the United States
95628LV00002B